MW01155129

UNBELIEVABLE STORIES OF
KOBE BRYANT

THIS BOOK BELONGS TO:

UNBELIEVABLE STORIES OF
KOBE BRYANT

INTRODUCTION

Regarded as one of the greatest basketball players of all time, Kobe Bryant spent most of his 20-year career with the Los Angeles Lakers. He was an 18-time All-Star and won 5 NBA championships during his career. Along with his teammate Shaquille O'Neal, he led the Lakers to three consecutive NBA championships from 2000-2002.

Off the court, Kobe pursued many other interests in music, film, television, business, and philanthropy. Throughout his extraordinary life, Kobe never stopped pushing himself to up his game because he believed whole-heartedly that hard work could take him anywhere. He certainly wasn't wrong.

Chapter 1:
Kobe in Italy

Kobe looked out the window as the plane rose into the sky. Philadelphia grew smaller and smaller. Kobe saw his dad, Joe "Jellybean" Bryant, lean back in his seat and close his eyes. He tried to do the same but his tummy squirmed with nerves. They were moving to Italy. A whole new country! Kobe wondered what it would be like. Would he like the food? Would he be able to talk to anyone? Finally, he leaned back and managed to fall into a fitful sleep.

"Passa la palla!" Kobe shouted. His teammate threw the ball. Kobe pounded down the court in the city of Reggio Emilia, Italy, speeding past his opponent. He was feeling so sure of himself that he stopped at the three-point line and took a shot. He held his breath. The shot careened off the hoop and out of bounds. Just then the game ended.

His teammates cheered. Despite the missed shot, they'd won. Kobe's teammate and friend, Dave, invited Kobe over to watch TV to celebrate the win. Kobe, sweat dripping down his face from the Italian heat, just shook his head.

"Don't be so hard on yourself," Dave said. "You're the best player on the team." Kobe shook his head again, "If I'm gonna make it to the NBA, I gotta be the best player in the world."

At 12-years-old, Kobe had been living in Italy for six years and was the best player on his youth basketball team, but he'd missed the shot today.

He got home, grabbed a snack, and took a basketball out to his home court. He felt the ball, familiar in his hand. He stood on the three-point-line and bounced it a few times before leaping in the air and shooting. He held his breath. Swoosh. Kobe smiled. "One down, one-hundred to go."

For the rest of the night, Kobe practiced his shot. With every swoosh, he saw in his mind's eye an image of himself in an NBA jersey. He heard in the distance as the crowd shouted his name: "Kobe! Kobe! Kobe!"

Chapter 2:
Kobe in High School

Kobe flashed a devilish grin as he snatched the ball from his friend and teammate, Jason. School had ended an hour ago, and they were finishing playing a one-on-one game in Lower Merion High School's gymnasium in Philadelphia. Before Jason had time to react, Kobe was already bouncing toward the net. He did an easy lay-up and the ball lazily dropped into the net.

"That's 100," Kobe shouted. "I win!" He turned around.

"Yeah, yeah, you win, Kobe." Jason was in the middle of the court, sweating and breathing heavily.

Kobe laughed. "Wanna go again?"

That night, Kobe traded his basketball shoes and jersey for a nice suit. He looked at himself in the mirror and felt strange. At only seventeen, he'd already been named to the All-American boys' team and landed a $2 million Adidas contract. Still, without a basketball in his hand, he was a little nervous.

At the awards, a few people took pictures with Kobe, but he was hardly the main event. All of a sudden, there was a bunch of chatter and Kobe turned to the entrance. The actress and singer, Brandy Norwood, had just entered the room. A bunch of photographers snapped her picture and she was immediately surrounded by fans. Kobe's mouth went dry and his hands became clammy. This was going to be harder than he thought.

Later in the night, Kobe saw Brandy again. This time she was standing alone, getting a drink of water.

"You miss 100% of the shots you don't take," he reminded himself. He took a deep breath and approached. "Hi."

"Hi," Brandy said back.

Kobe tried to think of something else to say but couldn't. Finally, he blurted out, "I'm a basketball player. That's why I'm here."

"Cool. I'm an actress and singer," Brandy replied.

"I know. I'm, um, a big fan."

"Thank you." Brandy finished drinking her water. "I should go back to my group," she said.

It was his last chance. Before he could think too hard about it, he said quickly, "Do you want to go to my prom with me?"

"Oh," Brandy said, surprised. Then she smiled at him. "Maybe. I have to check with my mom, but that sounds fun. I'll let you know."

Before Kobe could say anything else, Brandy was whisked away by another photographer. It didn't matter though. Whether she said yes or no, he'd gotten up the nerve to ask. He got home that night, grinning from ear to ear. A few months later, he showed up to prom with teen superstar Brandy Norwood on his arm. All because he'd had enough courage to ask.

Chapter 3:
The Youngest Player in an NBA All-Star game

Kobe couldn't believe it. At just 17 years old, he'd been drafted by the NBA! He was going to play on the Los Angeles Lakers. He learned that he was the first guard to ever be drafted right out of high school. His parents beamed at him proudly. They were about to sign his contract and then he'd officially be on the team. Because he was still a minor he couldn't sign it himself, but that hardly bothered him. Right before signing, his dad, Joe "Jellybean" Bryant, looked over at him, tears in his eyes. He had been a player in the NBA and was now watching his son follow in his footsteps.

"You're gonna work hard, aren't you, son?" Joe asked him, already knowing what the answer would be.

"Yes, sir," Kobe said. Joe picked up his pen and signed. His son was in the NBA.

Kobe watched his team from the bench, full of nerves. His legs bounced up and down. He wanted to be on the court, but he was still a rookie in his first season and the youngest player ever to play in an NBA game, so he didn't get a lot of playing time yet. Finally, his coach pointed at him and told him he was up. He jumped from his seat on the bench.

Once on the court, he was unstoppable. He was too quick for the defenders, who couldn't catch up to him. It was his very first game in the NBA, and he knew he needed to prove himself. A teammate passed him the ball and he leapt in the air, tossing the ball towards the net. He watched it drop into the basket with a satisfying swish. By the end of the game, he'd scored 25 points. His coach was thrilled. Kobe assured him, "I'm gonna get more next time." He wasn't lying.

Going into the Western Conference semifinals, Kobe was feeling good. He was still in his first season, but he was already making waves. So as the playoff game against the Utah Jazz started, he was confident. Until everything started to go wrong. Kobe watched a teammate get into a fight with another player and get kicked out. All of a sudden, Kobe was placed in a lead role in the game.

Despite his excitement, Kobe watched the time tick down and knew he'd have to go big to win. Yet each time he got ahold of the ball and took a shot, he'd watch the ball miss wildly. When the final buzzer went off, the Utah Jazz had won 98-93. The Lakers were eliminated.

As Kobe started to beat himself up over the missed shots, Shaquille O'Neal told him, "No one has the guts to take shots like that." He realized that risk was part of what made him the player he was. Just because it didn't always pay off, it didn't mean he should stop. He took a deep breath and turned his attention to the future. By his third season, he was the youngest player to start in an NBA All-Star game.

Chapter 4:
Kobe and Shaq Feud

K obe felt the blood pumping in his ears. He was mad. He knew trash talking was part of basketball, but he didn't expect it from his own teammate! They were in the middle of a scrimmage game, and Kobe and Shaq were playing opposite each other.

Kobe was a rookie and Shaq was a seasoned player, so he knew Shaq expected to win easily. As Kobe got possession of the ball and pounded his way towards the basket on the opposite end of the court, he heard Shaq hurl another insult in his direction, and before he could stop and think about it, he turned around and yelled at his 7'1", 300-pound teammate, "What'd you just say to me?"

The ball bounced off the court, forgotten, as the two players confronted each other. Shaq, who wasn't used to being challenged, let alone by a rookie, didn't take it well.

"Watch out, Kobe," a few teammates said. But Kobe wasn't about to back down. He walked up to Shaq, daring him to repeat his insults. Shaq decided to change course, instead throwing a punch at Kobe. Kobe was shocked but not for long. If his blood was pumping before, it was nothing compared to now. He immediately stood up and started to fight back. He saw Shaq's eye brows shoot up in surprise. He wasn't used to being challenged. The two continued to fight until finally, their teammates pulled them apart. They stomped off to the locker room, too angry to speak.

In the locker room, Kobe managed to cool down with a few deep breaths. He felt ashamed that he'd allowed Shaq to rile him up. They were supposed to be teammates. He felt the bench he was on lower a bit and saw Shaq had sat down next to him. Shaq looked at the floor as he spoke.

"Ya know, kid, you really held your own out there."

"It's Kobe," Kobe replied coldly.

"Kobe, it's not easy for me to admit when I'm wrong. I'm very competitive."

"Yeah, me too," Kobe replied.

"Maybe instead of fighting, we should try working together," Shaq said quietly.

Kobe softened. "I'd like that."

The two smiled and shook on it. Just like that, the competition between the two of them was forgotten.

At least for now. They didn't know it right then, but by agreeing to work together, these two powerhouse players would go on to win 3 championships together, making them one of the most beloved basketball duos of all time.

Chapter 5:
Kobe the Perfectionist

Beep, beep, beep. Kobe reached out one of his long arms and shut off his alarm clock. For most people, 4 am might still feel like the middle of the night. Kobe just hopped out of bed and felt his way towards the dresser so he could grab workout gear and socks. By 5 am, he was in the gym, shooting baskets and running drills by himself. In the dark. As he shot another basket, the lights suddenly went on.

Byron Scott, the head coach, said,

"Kobe, practice doesn't start for two more hours. What're you doing?"

"Getting better," Kobe said seriously. "I want to be the best."

On game day, Kobe still got up early to workout. As his teammates stumbled into the gym, rubbing sleep out of their eyes, they just shook their heads at an already sweaty Kobe. He saw their disbelief, but he didn't care. He knew it might look odd, but it was what worked for him.

"Yo, Kobe," one of his teammates said. "We have a game today. Why are you doing a full workout?"

"There's never a bad time to get better," Kobe said between pushups. "I want to be the best."

Later, in the locker room, the Lakers toweled sweat off their faces during half-time. Kobe immediately turned on the TV in the room and started watching the first half of the game. A few of his teammates groaned. He pointed at the video as an image of him missing a shot played.

"See that? If I'd gone the other way, I would've avoided getting stuck so far from the basket and I would've made the shot."

"C'mon, why do we gotta watch the game, Kobe? We just played it."

"Because," Kobe said, "we have to work to get better if we want to be the best."

Begrudgingly, his teammates gathered around and began watching the first half of their game with Kobe. They knew he was right, and they wanted to be the best.

Chapter 6:
Kobe and Music, Beethoven's Moonlight Sonata

Kobe couldn't believe his luck. Not only was he a rising star in the NBA, but Sony Entertainment was interested in producing his music. He felt like he was on top of the world, except for one small detail. His new single K.O.B.E. was about to debut, and he wasn't sure if it was quite right.

He had come from underground hip hop, but Sony Entertainment wanted his song to be more radio friendly, so he had made some changes. He brushed the thought away. Sony knew what it was talking about. They were music pros. He smiled in anticipation, feeling like he was on top of the world.

Kobe's cheeks burned red and he cringed. He was at the NBA All-Star Weekend and heard his new song K.O.B.E. come on again. How many times were they going to play it? It'd been out for almost a whole month, and the reviews had been awful. He felt embarrassed, but he just put his head down and kept practicing with his team.

Soon after the debut, Kobe got a call that made his stomach drop. Sony told him they no longer wanted to move forward with his full album. Kobe was crushed. He loved basketball, but he loved music too. One of his dreams looked like it was about to shatter.

Kobe sat down at a piano and put headphones in his ears. He rested his large hands on the keys. It had been more than 10 years since his single was released and flopped. Since then, he'd had a few small music successes, but nothing big. He'd had to let that dream go. He had a new mission now. This time the song wasn't for him or for his career. He wanted to learn to play Moonlight Sonata on the piano, and he wanted to do it for his wife Vanessa.

He pressed play and his headphones began playing Moonlight Sonata. The beautiful and melancholy tune made him tear up. He started practicing, attempting to pick out notes by ear. It was long and tedious. In fact, his fingers never seemed to hit the notes just right. He took a deep breath and tried again. He knew he could take lessons if he wanted, but he was determined to get it on his own and learn the song by ear. Self-teaching the song was a symbol of his love for Vanessa. His finger slipped again. He stretched his hand, took a deep breath, and started again.

When Vanessa eventually heard it, she listened to Kobe play in awe. Once again, he'd shown even those closest to him, the power of hard work and dedication.

Chapter 7:
Kobe Gets Injured

T ap-tap-tap. *Kick ball change.* *Tappity tap tap.* The summer after the 2012 season, Kobe Bryant, one of the most famous basketball players of all time, found himself in a tap class learning how to shuffle, kick ball change, and do the buffalo. As he finished up his class for the day, he toweled sweat off his brow. He smiled to himself. Today's tap class required that he learn a difficult combination, and he was proud that he'd finally nailed it. He sat down to untie his tap shoes. As he did, he admired the new muscles he could see building in his ankles and he thought back to what brought him to this tap class in the first place.

Bounce-bounce-bounce. Shoot. Swish. It all started during the 2012 season. Kobe was having a great game. He could feel the crowd watching him as he ran up and down the court. Their cheers pushed him harder towards the basket as he took possession of the ball. He was on top of the world when BAM! Pain shot through his ankle like he'd never experienced and he dropped to the floor. It was agonizing, but he knew the game wasn't over. A foul was called and he'd have to shoot two free throws.

One of his teammates helped him stand. "You okay, Kobe?" he asked. "That was a rough fall."

Kobe clenched his jaw and nodded. With help, he limped to the free throw line. He mustered everything he had in him and shot. The ball landed in the basket and the crowd went wild. He had one more. Again, he pushed through the pain, and, again, the ball landed in the basket. The crowd went wild. Barcly keeping from collapsing, Kobe left the court.

The doctor told him he'd ruptured his Achilles tendon. The injury was severe. The doctor shook his head sadly before telling Kobe, "This could take a year or more to fully recover."

Kobe was back in action in 8 months, healing his injury in record time. However, even after he'd healed, he was worried it wasn't enough...

Kobe faithfully followed the dance instructor, mastering the new combination for the day. All summer, he'd been taking tap lessons. It felt good to be getting better at the dance moves. He felt the muscles in his ankles getting stronger. He could feel his feet getting faster and his rhythm improving. He smiled and watched in the mirror as his feet went *tap-tap-tap. Kick ball change. Tappity tap tap.*

Chapter 8:
Kobe the Business Mogul

Kobe's blood was pumping and he was excited, but this time it wasn't about basketball. Though he was known as one of the greatest basketball players in the NBA and the world, he had found something that he was equally as passionate about: Business.

It was 3 o'clock in the morning and the light of his computer shined on his face as he studied the portfolio of BodyArmor, one of his most recent investments. Only a few short years ago he'd agreed to invest, putting $6 million dollars of his own money into the company. Now, four years later, his investment was worth $200 million. He thought back to why he'd been so drawn to BodyArmor...

In 2012, Mike Repole, the founder of BodyArmor, had been cautiously excited by Kobe's enthusiasm for the company. Kobe was used to people reacting this way to his intense interest and didn't let it bother him.

He told Mike, "I want BodyArmor to be number one, and I want to help make it happen."

"Kobe, I have to be honest with you. Only one out of 100 brands make it. We have a 1 percent chance," Mike told him.

Kobe just smiled his most winning grin and replied, "Want to guess the odds for becoming an NBA player?"

UNBELIEVABLE STORIES OF KOBE BRYANT

Over the next few years, Kobe Bryant wasn't content to sit on the sidelines. Just like he did with basketball, he worked hard to understand everything he could about how to improve the company he believed in. His Mamba Mentality was all about the pursuit of self-improvement. Kobe knew if he learned everything he could about business, he could help the company grow.

He represented the company as an athlete who believed in the product. Not only did his own investment grow, but BodyArmor went from $3 million in sales in 2012 to nearly $200 million by 2017.

Although, as per usual, this wasn't enough for Kobe Bryant. BodyArmor was a product he believed in, and he wanted to make it the number one sports drink on the market, above Gatorade and Powerade. While BodyArmor hasn't yet reached Kobe's goal, it was Kobe's belief that he could always get better that made him strive for what others thought was impossible. For him, with enough time and hard work, the impossible often became reality.

Chapter 9:
Kobe Wins an Oscar

Sitting down at his desk, Kobe pulled out a black ink pen and stared down at the blank white sheet in front of him. He had so many thoughts swirling around in his head. An ice pack on his shoulder, the latest injury he'd endured, dripped water down his arm as it slowly melted. The 2015–16 season, his 20th season with the Lakers, was about to begin. As he felt the aches and pains that come with over two decades of pushing his body to the limit, he took a deep breath. He knew what he had to do. He pressed his pen to the top of the page and wrote the words, "Dear Basketball." So began the poem that would announce his retirement from his first and biggest love: Basketball.

As fans poured into the Staples Center at the beginning of the 2015–16 season, Kobe's palms began to sweat. He'd already published his poem "Dear Basketball." The news was out that he was retiring, but he didn't yet know how it would be received by the fans. In his poem, he'd written:

This season is all I have left to give
My heart can take the pounding
My mind can handle the grind
But my body knows it's time to say goodbye

When the crowd had finally entered for the first game of the season, they stood up and cheered for Kobe. He let the cheers wash over him, tears springing to his eyes. In the crowd, he saw and heard the voices of his fans as they thanked him for the years he'd dedicated to the team. Then began the first game of the final season of his career.

Restless as ever, Kobe's retirement didn't slow him down at all. Now that his basketball career had ended, he decided to set his sights on a new dream. He wanted to turn his poem "Dear Basketball" into an animated short film. So he did.

Kobe reached out to Glen Keane, a director who worked on Disney films, and John Williams, a well-known composer, and the team worked on creating a film that would allow Kobe to fully realize his emotional goodbye to the game he loved.

The next time he heard the cheers from the crowd it wasn't because he'd scored another incredible basket. It was because his name had just been called from a dazzling podium. He stood from his plush red seat and made his way towards the stage. Kobe Bryant's film "Dear Basketball" had just won an Oscar.

From basketball star to star filmmaker, Kobe had once again set his mind to a task and excelled beyond anyone's wildest imagination.

Chapter 10:
Kobe's Philanthropy and his Legacy

Kobe entered the home of eight-year-old Jeffrey McKenzie, who was currently hiding behind the legs of his mother. Kobe knew the young boy had sickle cell anemia and that he might be a little weak or shy, so he entered cautiously. However, as soon as the boy saw him, he let out a squeal of joy and ran towards Kobe who caught him in his arms just in time. The boys eyes shined with joy.

"You're my hero," he told Kobe shyly.

He looked over at little Jeffrey's mom. She had tears in her eyes. "You don't know how much this means to us," she told Kobe through her tears. Kobe looked down at the little boy who was fighting a battle against his own body, a battle Kobe both could and couldn't imagine. He looked back up at his mother and said, "With all due respect, you have no idea what it means to me either."

In the course of his career, Kobe would grant more than 100 wishes for the Make-A-Wish foundation.

Kobe knew he was a good problem solver. On the court or off, when he saw a problem that needed fixing, he wanted to be the one to do it.

"It's not just about being the best at basketball," he told his wife, Vanessa as they sat in their home in Los Angeles. "I had so much opportunity growing up. Make-A-Wish is wonderful, but I need to do more. I need to be the best human I can be."

"What do you want to fix, Kobe?" Vanessa asked him.

"Everything," he told her. "Cancer, homelessness, youth enrichment for the underprivileged."

"If you were anyone else, I'd say you're crazy to take all of that on," she said. "But you're Kobe Bryant. I think you can do anything you put your mind to. So, where do you wanna start?"

He smiled. "I've got some ideas."

In 2007, Kobe and Vanessa Bryant launched the Kobe and Vanessa Family Foundation. Kobe was proud of his organization, which helped sponsor international enrichment experiences for minority college students. He would go on to also work with organizations that helped combat youth homelessness, because he found young people to be incredibly inspiring.

If Kobe Bryant had only ever played basketball, he would still be remembered as a legend for simply being one of the greatest NBA players of all time. Perhaps his greatest accomplishment though, was his willingness to always push himself to do more. Basketball made him a star. His heart, mind, and work ethic made him immortal.

THE END

CPSIA information can be obtained
at www.ICGtesting.com
Printed in the USA
BVHW021924021221
623107BV00006B/185